Shifting Tides

Shifting Tides

Carroll Blair

Aveon Publishing Company

Copyright © 2012 by Carroll Blair

New Edition

All rights reserved. No part of this book may be reproduced or transmitted in any form or by any means, electronic or mechanical, including photocopy, recording, or by any information storage and retrieval system without prior permission of the publisher.

ISBN: 978-1-936430-22-2

Library of Congress Control Number
2012920983

Aveon Publishing Co.
P.O. Box 380739
Cambridge, MA 02238-0739 USA

Also by Carroll Blair

Grains of Thought
Facing the Circle
Reel to Real
Reaches
Quarter Notes
Out of Silence
By Rays of Light
Into the Inner Life
Gnosis of the Heart
Soul Reflections
Beneath and Beyond the Surface
Of Courage and Commitment
For Today and Tomorrow
In Meditation
Sightings Along the Journey
Through Desert's Fire
Offerings to Pilgrims
Human Natures
(Of Animal and Spiritual)
Atoms from the Suns of Solitude
Colors of Devotion
Voicings

Contents

I

Footnotes	15
What More	16
Silent Moon Puppy	17
X L R 8	18
In Crowned Defeat	19
Saranade	20
Out to Out	21
Ground Innocence	22
Nick of Time	23
In Deed Unspoken	24
Miss in Formation	25
Tainted Sonorities	26
Falling Away	27
Angel of Incapacity	28
Trial Pedestrians	29
World Without	30
Pi Without Center	31
Curious Thing	32
Still Lying	33
Fare Play	34
Gray to Blue	35
To One	36

II

What Not	39
Hearts	40
Brother's Turnaround	41
Boxed Man	42
Portrait	43
Summer Scene	44
Cousin to Cousin	45
Their Odds and Rebels Too	46
World Pressing On	47
Hotel Isolate	48
Of Humans Most	49
Quiz zz	50
None of the Above	51
Emotions All	52
Somehow Someway	53
All the Time	54
Fateless Vision	55
Nature – Understanding	56
An Artist's Request on His First Visit to Club Muse	57
Both Sad and Happy Day	58
Waves	59
High North in the Dead of Winter	60
Santa Claus Ringing a Bell Outside a Shopping Mall the Day After Thanksgiving	61
To Advertise	62
Passing the Buck	63
Sold	64
Hostage Held	65
No Questions Asked	66

III

One Day Sing	69
With Open Arms	70
The Best Within Not Always Discovered	71
Solo Traveller	72
How It Happens	73
One Plus One	74
Depending on How It Is Viewed	75
For Another to Another	76
Between the Lines	77
In Silence	78
Something to Consider	79
Fool for Power	80
Old Man T	81
Take Two	82
So Too the Rains of Life	83
Awareless	84
Excerpt from a Letter from Ex-Student to Ex-Mentor	85
Pressure Peer	87
Lonely One	88
Wind	89
One Day No More	90
By Law of Nature	91
Before the Grave	92
Cross Gathering	93
Final Briefing to World War ll Pilots on Their Final Mission	94
A Child's Question	95
Eavesdrop on a Lordly Debate	96
In This Human Race	97

Earthquakes of a Life	98
In – Sight	99
Fears	100
Reactionary Lives	100
Birth of Spiritual Knowledge	101
Not Always So Gently	102
The Spruce and the Pear Tree	103
At a Reading	104
What Might the Greatest Poem Be?	105
Reunion	106

I

Footnotes

Bold, — cold, — brutal to the files of flawful history
tombed in baled artifice beneath time not shown
to anyone of late, pressed by Falsehood taunting,
circling, summoning the ides of foreboding
pulling lost tales into the bully of Now believing
the legend of Progress, the prime of conversion
trumpeting the call that tucks them all
gamely in their fraud so safe in their
disease, spreading at will to present day
forged lore of flaw-filled history.

What More

A cluster of mad biologies; a lie squirming in the grass . . .
a phase out of bounds behind the field of Lost Count
arguing the price of life with a burglar waving studied
hands . . . a fractured nuance trimmed to the satisfaction
of magicians shooting sails into the sky without a care
or knows who why, exploding memorials by the light
of blue harbors polishing apertures with the blessing of
yesterday's dawn . . .

and what more could a rain-sun want or ask for

Silent Moon Puppy

Silent moon puppy taking the heat for your circumstance
in ways fleeting past the surface lobes of mind
absorbed in understandings critical to all fours and the
nothing-to-do-with-you-s brash in bond findings
the spot where you placed your paw, where you'll
one day bury your bones calming the waves of viscerals
sending traces out to sea braving the light's stamina
gearing to its end riding the goal of direction, the beam
steady-as-she-goes down to its last sigh not even a flicker
stunting your poise, cast in wild and free
oh silent moon puppy . . .   how earth and star salute you

X L R 8

A neuroblast megaton unknown exploded forcefully inside a puzzle working its way toward bedlam derelict in its duty of collision pieced together frame by frame, a vision of throbbing fingers fixed to a creaseless band stretching in the wrong direction portioning cracked verticals abiding by law vying for the picture of blow-by-blow description in scrambling overhaul as Comfort soured the antics of Cope carving a messy scene for the queen of Nobody Knows clutching fines in the palms of her prayers for mercies shown the base of the unexplored reaching through depths of horrible-far preying without disturbance, seizing the ground of gnome-play gliding sane to a standstill casting in cynical the riddle of blind faith rolling out of itself into the field of Mind Everlasting

In Crowned Defeat

The day saps itself clean . . . missions to fulfill . . . body changes grown to immense yearnings halted at the door of Collide . . . island testimonies cradle their newborns shown the primal force unto themselves hemmed in clocked perception reaching for ables punishing to all standards adorned, charmed to the miracles that beseech in warring spells waiting to seize the noon passing through quarters safe in their removal, riding the alternative to why it all must be in feigned de-light lifting the final reflection to the day forever raising what it is not . . .
forever damning what it is   it is   what is . . .

Saranade

Sun-laid particles everywhere . . . do you see them, Sara,
dusting the walks of princes there in your garden in ways
not told by anyone yet to believe the reason for your
acceptance sparing the cross cutting your hands bolting
hours pruned to the minute (you do expect to be delivered
don't you) on something strict like cheese in a Ninja's diet
(there were visions you would behave this way) . . .
dread is the sighing of angels noting crimes in pads
without lines or color to be rehearsed then destroyed by
Cicero's way (the breadth of your motion is stunning)
setting dreams to fire by rule of ancient Sundays

Out to Out

Putting yourself out to out of touch beyond mines of fineless fees, hard so hard for the as-king . . . sounds ripping forward to ring outstanding in the incurve's folding scene for reasons striking out to prove us wrong

and if the day knows that what else for there to know

Ground Innocence

Of straight and narrow climbs touched like rivers frameless
in their flow through reachings tantamount to cross phrases
bellowing forks tuned to the music of the stars
shifting temperatures absent in the measure of all things
railing scope through seals primed maximus like bond
to fire fielding murmurs of 'why I wish to tell you-s'
mounting the arc of decibel-freeze by force and reconcile
cluttering the known with seed of the unexpected
moving ground innocence to turn   to
rise   to free

Nick of Time

Fast to the nick of time to witness Time prowl about and
laugh in dire scorn at all who fail to see its self-inflicted
cuts and bruises taunting in cruel absurdities its measure
bound to invisible fate losing nothing in a stream of
murdered moments bursting in hints of a
fading proof that they exist at all
that their mother truly is . . .
that they truly are

In Deed Unspoken

Bending over lean and viable, sweeping stories away from
places and whispers perilous to the victims left on the floor
of a novelist's suite and old songs of mending
mapping a courtyard fit for something warm and sassy
holding a halo in its drum, holding passwords revisited,
revised, certain of the fame it will cause and choking every
sliver of it, trolling for transient shifts shy to adventure
and gypsies without shoes or sight finding the porter
bending over his dream, watching clean and bountiful
with courage in deed unspoken

Miss in Formation

Spilling over a score print of clues missed in formation
set for maydays farthest to the faraway speakers
spinning lime with the fakers of crime

some said fool-a-day, some saw fossil-gray, worn to a
sci-fi hilt, to a crossways fit for the bone dust
blowing over the mountain holding an onion in its crust
frantic for its peace and a vulpine-sure

paining an observer filled with love and empty
capturing the moment on a matchbook before it slips away

Tainted Sonorities

moving in dark places, soldiered in glass spaces reeling from the jar of their course . . . a masked fury surprises with a gracious gesture streaming half-phrases between the bars of its prison coiled in a serpent's watch, its stare carried in kind to young shadows bowering fictions assailed by a morning's wind too cold to crash the mood of grate expectancy singing to the rocks that haven't moved for centuries, waiting to shine like stars

Falling Away

making way for the big-boxed tuba blasting in burps
summoning the verdict of That's All billing messengers
polished in their privacy growing restless for the
challenge they've been sold pitching clay miracles
into the well of No Retreat letting nothing get away with
Nothing forcing laughter from a monk evicted from below
rising in crayoned fits marking the walls on his way out
drawing streets from memory where the bulls ran with
the sheep in scars of euphoria peaking half-crazy before
the silver city of Soon lighting afar not far beyond the
counting of the ways life leaves everything undone
to be trampled and scattered about in sweeps of ash
prodding the wounds of dare-seekers seasoned in
their stride smirking at the faceless braving streams
of satisfactions looped to the center of themselves
sheltered as a tree house shut away in the woods
where animals and graded children tell their secrets
falling on blades of stone

Angel of Incapacity

What is it that paints itself black with brush invisible
lighting candles without wicks, shooting stars as
fast as they are born drawn holy to the fireball
all infused with remnants of desolate matter, bare
elements scratching the muzzle of Blind in mystery
cold so beautifully cold, unspeakably kind in its cruelty
to be of itself holding like the calm servant of IS in
perfected oblivion marching manifests to their graves
traceless in their manner of pace shaping venues by
hysteria crumbling before a Quaker's fall quick to
begin so slow to end in synchronized hope framing
pictures not yet visioned, sounding songs not yet sung
for an age yet to behold erecting barriers outside the cage
of isolation bleeding tears not shaming themselves not
purposing themselves by criteria of something new to
importance condemned to a reign of sensories to be for
now a burning yes to All and all things that have waited
to introduce themselves and sign with gallant warning to
the angel of incapacity painting itself black with brush
invisible, guarding sacrifice now bound and unspoken
setting in chamber without cover or light as all
who have yet to wake from consciousness
the hounds barking at the door

Trial Pedestrians

Trial pedestrians out for a walk strolling through summer feasts touring the city sun, stepping on heat approaching the zero hour saved for sum-day afternoons . . . they say the resurrection is near . . . whole surroundings stitch pieces together anticipating Forever flashing in neon with carpets spread from park to coast leasing villagers of coming nations to chair the event reaching through blinds of color-kindness offering themselves to a prophet who refuses to wait, handing his epitaph hand to wing to the nightingale determined to sing its song through the cage of still-tomorrows.

World Without

Rape on the stairs —

Murder in the hallway —

Bishops seated on the floor playing Russian roulette with the morning's immigrants —

Children eating breakfast at the dinner table, their mother in the kitchen preparing lunch for school —

Nothing extraordinary; nothing unusual —

Harriet without Ozzie,
the world without Oz

Pi Without Center

For the pi without center forcing lone geometries to take turns for the worst, jumping to algebraized Ys and U2s (O Y O Y) I give you weak's equationings useless in their manners, juvenile in their schemes and an X (of course) to mark the spots of wholes not whole by in-betweens, trashing the aisles through A to Z

Curious Thing

Oh those stretchings and reachings into the unknown with hands of mind and eyes of heart, searching for anything near resembling the aura of Truth . . . Mystery grinning in the dark inviting one, inviting all who inner journey to earn a flash of its light, a peek at its story with that curious thing that killed the curious cat

Still Lying

Captured in rapturous detail, the motion of a frog saying it all, spilling it all in its croaking manner of taste given to the faithful spinning the scene loosely like the spin doctor looking for the hook to place his bait upon lying beside the snake in the grass lying still, hidden beneath the sun without notice, lying . . . .   still lying

Fare Play

The hour obscure in its time fielding shots of frail moments
seeping into the silo of Promise bled, masking that portion
of the way that screams enough! in resigned terror
watching with bearded eyes a boy wandering in the street
thinking of nothing but the earth covering his knees
and what this will cost him when he returns h o m e

Gray to Blue

Crowned leaps in shadowed feet crossed bearings unread
heard massing in form rearing to mount in kind, scaling to
a realm castled in bands of gold and white tripping the wind
raw and tameless splendid as the day when nothing is said
carting green wheels to a hillside waiting for the caw of
the crow that draws swiftly to the ending of something
soon to begin, tracing beaches in forests of snow
beneath a sky clearing itself gray to blue,
lifting the eagle heading for home.

To One

I heard the church bells; I know of the sermon
delivered with tears years from the grace of its offering
and the woman praying for the souls of her daughters
and those of sires unknown — I saw the child sleeping
by the altar — I know of the rosary left in the pew by
the soldier forty years home I saw the postman delivering
flyers to the entrance with no name and the saints
driving by slowly stopping only to pick up nails; I saw
the light fading on the steps shading the distant grove,
I saw you leaving alone going to the plains of harvest-hope
without pails or pigtails with love in your hands
caressing the air dancing gently above the ground and
moving all around you, certain to lead you to yourself
to the story of yourself singing to the guardians of your
mind "all in good time" finding the road that won't desert
you, that you deserted so long ago in fragments now re-
moved from blessings shielding the wounds of your heart
lighting the presence that folds within and curls without,
giving the flowers a run for their sun finding its way back
to you   to where   to here . . .   to one

II

What Not

A slaughterhouse was preparing for its best,
readying for the worst outside itself, beside itself
projecting the light that herds its victims to its
doors — some rats some devils some whores
stepping in twos, some carrying their tots —

Noah's ark it was not

Hearts

drawn to the matter of jamming Life in the throat —
the way is cleaner than the result, the fault
lying with Interpretation
headstrong in its lifelong battle with invisibles
dominating the landscapes of loveolution and sexolution

Brother's Turnaround

Morphing in quick turnaround reaching sore into the nest
of foil-soothing grained in spells half-natural sounding dial-
a-mean for the blinds your neighbor gave you in cowed
measure, recalling the time you smiled and bid him good
morning his dog's ass still tingling from your boot
the day sunny yes bright shining

Boxed Man

Sitting in his stand selling his newspapers and magazines the man gray and gray, looking at his customers' chests, their hands their waists their knees, anywhere but in their eyes, speaking no words receiving and changing currency as business dictates, stone-faced cold without expression all connection to humanity gone without a trace.

Someone said she heard him once, just once, long ago say something like   "Have a nice day."

Portrait

The birdhouse yesterday stationed in a tree held by
two ropes hung from a branch in perfect symmetry
is today hanging from one rope, the other rope slack
the birdhouse now vertical, its entrance faced
to the sky swaying slightly from side to side
moving in the air like a hanged man

Summer Scene

Pennies crushed on the track, flat — now faceless copper
shining in the sun, the train leaving the scene of the crime
set by two laughing boys howling at each other
"It could be you!" "It could be you!!"
leaving the copper without face, without circle
adding another two cents for the next train approaching
faster, more eager than the iron monster before

Their little sisters waiting with their quarters
watching from the bush

Cousin to Cousin

Try anything you like;
oh do indeed, by All and all means . . .
pursue any goal that tickles your fancy,
that fires your soul —

Just don't be a dime a dozen, cousin

Their Odds and Rebels Too

A flock of birds fly by and there are two not quite flying with the group, a little behind or ahead, a bit wide on one side, then the other side, one off to the right, another to the left . . . and the herds of animals . . . the elephant, the antelope, the zebra, the caribou . . . always one or two, sometimes more, not quite stepping with the group, ignoring the other members of the herd, more or less, moving at their own pace in their own way in a style that stands out from the rest, and I see from this and other examples of individuality, of stronger-than-species personality throughout the animal world that've caught my eye on more occasions than a few, that the animals indeed have their odds and rebels too.

World Pressing On

The world came pressing into his pores with hideous disease — blood rushing to their defense; — a weak warrior this time around in its flow . . . the red river usually thick with courage failing *this* time on *this* day to *this* life in its dutiful manner of dispensing with death threats moving against the force for which it lives, for which it flows —

the world pressing on

Hotel Isolate

— rooms for loners to rent by the hour or by life —
nothing in between where everything wavers in the
cracks of in-betweens — complaints about the heat,
always the heat . . . for most, too much — the rooms
just too damn hot — but the rare ones, the rarest of
the lone ones . . . they alone stay an hour and never return —
the heat for them not hot enough

Of Humans Most

Two dogs jump in the air to try and snatch the balls their masters hold in their hands — one jumps because he really wants the ball; the other, perhaps more intelligent (but according to the following must also in a manner be less) jumps to please his master in his silly game of tease — one, slave to his own desires — the other, slave to the desires of another.

Sounds something like the behavior of some humans . . .

(of humans many

. . . of humans most)

Quiz zz

1. Does anyone love you?

2. If yes, why does he or she love you?

3. Are you sure that's the reason?

4. Do you love anyone?

5. If so, is it the person (or persons) who love you?

6. Why do you love him — her — them?

7. Are you sure that's the reason?

8. Elaborate further on #7.

9. State your opinion of #8.

10. Think again about question #1.

None of the Above

What would you do if everything in your life suddenly started to crack like a glass that's been insulted by water, its temperature too high? Would you dig yourself a hole then pray for weeds to cover you hoping in the meantime to shoo the horror away with your shivers? Or throw yourself in front of a truck? Or ask a cabdriver for a ride to the bridge? Or run through the streets screaming for help hoping that at least a van for the mad would take notice of you? Or buy a gun and save the world some trouble (or perhaps cause it some trouble)? Or boldly increase the temperature of the water (i.e. your life) and play chicken with the powers that be? Or stand still in the center of yourself and hope that Life would forget you (at least for a while), or would you call the news stations and tabloids and invite them to the most spectacular sky dive they will ever see?
What would you do?

What *would* you do . . .

(What

would

you

do

?)

Emotions All

in the heart
sprouting from
the same root
joined together
like a thorny bush

Somehow Someway

With pins in her mouth she went about the chore of
hemming her daughter's dress, daughter standing straight
but not still (though not a little girl anymore) . . .
mother deep in concentration dedicated to her commitment
to aid her daughter in the evening's event most important to
her, but *ouch!*   *hold still!*   *my leg!*   *my lip!*
will be heard several times before the task is through . . . .
a little blood drawn now and then between mother and
daughter one way or another . . .   no way to avoid
this ritual

All the Time

Into the path of the crow flies the butterfly
that will be eaten by the crow . . .
something beautiful sacrificed
to sustain the life
of something not as beautiful
nor as graceful or noble in
what it has inspired —

In Nature as in human life . . .

It happens all the time

Fateless Vision

He knew what was expected of him; the boy in the uniform suit dreaming of his life just barely begun, pulled this way and that by just about everyone (or so it appeared to his young mind). Embittered by the presumptions of his elders who were in no way his betters, and his classmates who were no way his peers never tiring of trying to cram their perversities into his heart, he performed his duties with gritting teeth saved by the belief that one day he would escape the folly and vulgarity that so repulsed him; would free himself from the coarse banalities of these bourgeois mediocrities. Someday; someday, he said, I will be free of all this.

He is now head salesman of a clothing store with a wife and two kids.

Nature – Understanding

A teenaged male and female in biology class glance at each other in the middle of a lecture — he notices the slit of her skirt, she the rise in his pants —

they understand everything

An Artist's Request on His First Visit to Club Muse

A glass of goodness please . . .

Yuchhh! Is *that* what it tastes like?

Give me a shot of evil on the rocks —

ahhhh . . . . That's more like it

Both Sad and Happy Day

. . . like when a school of thoughts pass through the mind
like a school of fish and you're only able to nab a few,
having no net using only cerebral fingers
so many swimming away forever . . . but the ripples and
waves pulsing through the brain as they make their
escape — a sensation not soon to be forgotten . . . and the
few captured thoughts flapping in the mind set down to
paper . . . a permanent reminder of that sad and happy day
when maybe (just maybe) the big one got away

Waves

Calling waves unbroken, steadily calling
one following the next in rapid succession
moving by force invisible —

Father said they're coming by his command.

Son said "Not so Papa (can't fool me!)
the wind is pushing from behind driven by an angel."

They end their lives on the dock splashing both
father and son leaving them soaking wet

High North in the Dead of Winter

Days of thirty below zero in the north, deep in the dead of winter not a bird in sight as expected, then a day's reprieve of thirty above and a pair of birds fly by and the thought crosses the mind: Aren't you two supposed to be in Florida, or the Caribbean, or somewhere else vacationing?

Santa Claus Ringing a Bell Outside a Shopping Mall the Day After Thanksgiving

Oh   Ho   Ho   Ho

          Ho   Ho   Ho

  Ho   Ho

      Ho

         Ho

             Ho

(Suckers . . . . !)

To Advertise

above and beyond the call of beauty,
calling to sisters and daughters and mothers to
step up and have a look at a page full of lookers
fashioned to a hilt in size and overkill,
shaming their waists and hips, their buttocks and
breasts, telling them *this you should be should want
to be oh yes, must really be just have to be* . . .

This not beautiful, Madison Avenue . . .

not beautiful

Passing the Buck

So many passing the buck these days
passing it in a hurry, no balls to take responsibility,
put it in their pocket and let the buck chew a hole in it —
perhaps chew a little flesh . . . maybe sculpt some real balls

Sold

Dressed in their business best hoping the worst for their
rivals, using every ounce of energy to get the better of all
competitors — to seize the advantage, take the initiative . . .
egos and ambitions colliding in full force like beasts in a rut
furiously bidding before the final bell, the arena always full,
always giving a show of clowns and monkeys
fighting over peanuts while selling their souls
for gold.

Hostage Held

Smoke spewing from plants, steadily rising from their stacks
forming toxic clouds riding over cities and towns held
hostage, exchanging the health of their residents for their
daily bread —

Jobs   Jobs   Jobs . . .

The CEOs say it's a good deal —

The Governors and Mayors agree . . .
your health tomorrow for your bread today —

Hey Joe, it's the American way

No Questions Asked

To the foot of his lawn he moves walking quickly,
having seen his newspaper delivered, dropped
onto his property; the sure-of-his-world neighbor
picking up his morning pleasure, the prized
pedestrian scroll rolled in circular shape as if
it were holding fish from the market.
With a bounce in his stride he steps back to his door
joyfully anticipating the coming of his morning ritual
his hot coffee and cold cereal on the table, this time
to himself before beginning his day enjoyed so much,
holding stories and opinions of the confusions of the
world in his hands the ink smudging his fingers
as he turns the pages, the feel of the paper
between them almost as great a pleasure as
having its words enter into his head
esp. the words of deadline scribblers
no questions asked.

III

One Day Sing

A cloud drifts by above empty houses
riding the breath of the sky, holding the lightning

in its breast that is yet to come
as a mother holds her hope in the sanctum of her womb

carrying the life that will one day sing its song,
reveal its power

bold like a solitary stone holding its ground
as the mountain falls into the sea

With Open Arms

Seated in a corner of an empty room, sitting beneath the clock waiting for its guest to return from his morning saunter taken alone, in solitude always the chair sits ready to receive the one nearing the round of his journey, the world of his mind forming new thoughts, creating new pictures and dreams to be mused and amuse upon his return, the chair waiting with open arms

The Best Within Not Always Discovered

like one being followed by a would-be lover
not known to him
completely unknown, following him all his life long
never revealing herself
never expressing her love pure and sweet
a love never to be tasted,
to be experienced —
the true love of his life   never to him known

Solo Traveller

The Voyager probe — solo craft journeying into
the deep space of the solar system where no one
or thing connected with earth or man has ventured before,
taking pictures and collecting data of a strange new world
out there alone, the metal craft doing its thing,
doing what it was made for

and too

the solo travellers of mind and spirit journeying into
the far reaches of human-being collecting data along
their travels to record and send out into the world
for whoever may listen, going their way alone
going to places never gone before, doing
(it seems) what they were made for

How It Happens

Beliefs cluttering young minds, invading young lives
few of them invited, the majority brought by adults
driven into their youth, brought every day, for many days
for months for years, then one day they finally stay
make themselves at home, move in for good
no longer noticed, no longer thought of as
something foreign, just part of the cerebral landscape —

for all but a free-spirited few, their presence now permanent
from which there's no escape —

One Plus One

One plus one equals two. Yes — the most basic lesson
in arithmetic — but oh how many fail, never learn
never master the most basic lessons of life,
living in a mode of one plus one plus one
plus one plus one . . . . . never reaching the equals . . .
never grasping the plus

Depending on How It Is Viewed

How Life punishes when one loses faith . . . .

or Truth rewards

For Another to Another

Man — changing one mask for another,
jumping from one pretense to another
like children jumping from stone to stone
to stepping stone, faces above the water
bottoms to the mud, surrounded by crocodiles
waiting for a fall

Between the Lines

All the words between the lines —
the speech in the silent pauses of speech . . .
All that's been said in all the unsaid that
ever was between beings human . . .

What tales to be told, what secrets to be revealed
singing to deaf ears   dancing naked before blind eyes

In Silence

"Your love is too weak to sustain me!"

What the misanthrope screams to humanity

Something to Consider

No one likes their food burnt to a crisp,
be it food for the body, the mind, or the spirit.

Something to consider for the in-your-face
fanatical preacher —

Fool for Power

There once was a man who built a house then
burned it down, planted some trees then chopped
them to the ground, built a boat then rigged it to explode,
cropped a field then poisoned its yield . . . always
planting and building, planting and building —
everything to eventually be destroyed. His wife and
mother of three asked him why he did these things;
he replied without skipping a beat: "Because of the
power it gives me, that I give to myself . . . the control
over life and death, over being and non-being;
makes me feel strong, invincible, mighty, like a king";
then grabbed his gun and went looking for his sons —
his wife shot him dead at the door.

Old Man T

Old man T was mean, was ornery . . . just as mean and ornery as a man could be — at least twice as evil as everyone else (i.e. everyone he knew and who knew him). No one could meet a more disagreeable fellow, a more odious or malevolent being. But then the damnedest thing happened — he awoke one morning with the crazy notion to do something nice for somebody . . . it felt good to him, so he did it again, then again . . . he kept on doing it till, without noticing or being motivated by a conscious desire for redemption, most of his evil had vanished, most deeds of an evil nature redeemed, leaving everyone else now twice as evil as he.

Take Two

A tiger was running through an open field being
pursued by a native from a nearby village running
behind him, chasing him down, or so it appeared.
Those who witnessed the event thought to themselves
how brave, how courageous this man must be,
until they saw another tiger running behind him.

So Too the Rains of Life

Walking in her yard after the storm deep in thought,
a woman far from blue passed under a tree at the
same time a wind came rushing in from the east
shaking water from the leaves, catching her off guard
taking her by surprise, the storm she thought she had
missed by staying indoors caught her with its echo
the sky then clear and dry, even the sun shining bright
teaching her that when it rains it can pour,
even when the rain is no more —

and so too the rains of life

Awareless

Loved one ... standing there in your vanity so prim and
proud, as confident as one can be, unaware that your gifts
are now waning, fast now fading away ... leaving you,
abandoning the prime of your being, but your pride
remaining as if nothing's happened, as if all remains
the same   can you not

sense your weakening powers, the downward spiralling
change? I'll love you anyway; will support you just the
same but shame   for shame ...

your pride still strong, remaining,
your gifts now fading away

Excerpt from a Letter from Ex-Student to Ex-Mentor

... yes, I know what is troubling you, confused with your identity dealing with crisis upon crisis, not understanding yourself or what this life is about, up one moment and down the next, unaware that we are but a pool of wandering consciousness probing a world more distant than near that cares nothing for us, that never mourns when you lose or applauds when you win; a reality harder for most to bear than the effort that goes into sustaining the illusion that it ain't so, that you do matter and the world is in your corner, unable to see or face or believe the truth of life's indifference ... born into a world without permission (your permission) trapped in a web of internal and external chaos from your first crying breath, never sustaining the same identity or content of being for more than a moment, never holding the same thought, the same emotion in head and heart *the identical thought or emotion* in all dimensions of color and tone *identical* for more than a moment, therefore never being the same person for more than ... (well, you know) though figments of mind make it seem so ... So we are really nothing, really, but a series of identities that go as quickly as they come, like waves rising and falling in the sea leaving one nothing to hold on to but the illusions that make life possible, that would not be bearable without believing that you are what you are not and things that you are not to keep you from realities that would bring Hercules to his knees take him to the mat, move him to the edge of madness . . . no, dear mentor; you and I and he and she and they and all who pass before you are neither this nor that for more than a flash, selves born then vanishing going as quickly as they birth into being, carried away like leaves in a mocking wind the ego distorting everything, creating pictures of identity that do not exist, but enough for now about this. So how's the new house, the old career, the new mistress, your wife Mable and the identical twins . . .

Pressure Peer

You offered me your flower, which I refused —
blind with hurt that I rejected your gift
you failed to notice my flower to you,
which was my refusal

Lonely One

Oh a mistake it is, letting just anyone touch your heart . . . so many hands unclean — spiritual hands — calloused, bruised without a stroke of love or sensitivity (I mean the real thing); but they disguise as best they can as something other than they are, so often succeeding — the fear of being alone behind it all, usually, letting anyone approach, inviting them in, believing that any company is better than none —

Not so . . .   oh not so   dear lonely one

Wind

The only invisible of Nature

that freely gives

itself away

One Day No More

From the shore he scans the ocean, a boy beyond his years though still in his child, scanning the waters with hesitant wonder thinking of the hour when he will be no more . . .

a gull flies overhead

the sun fades behind a cloud

the ocean kissing his feet

By Law of Nature

A worm once crawled onto the back of a sleeping eagle believing that he would discover what it was like to soar into the face of the sun with fearless power and grace. While the eagle slept the worm reflected on how grand his experience would be, growing with excitement and anticipation . . . but then the eagle awoke, stood and spread his wings, and as he prepared to take flight, the worm quickly crawled from his back back onto the ground, realizing that he had neither the courage nor the right to experience things that were beyond his nature.

They both then went their way; the eagle into the sky, the worm back into the earth.

Before the Grave

All stand before the graves of their lives . . .

some with eyes closed and trembling hands,

others with eyes open and steady,

all too steady hands

Cross Gathering

On cold nights mid-millennium
the crowds gathered to warm themselves
by the fires set for heretics and infidels,
not only warming their bodies but
also the lusting cruelty of their souls
the clergy watching from their balconies
whispering Latin for those who were burning —

'Twas they [dear priests] who supplied the feast.

Final Briefing to World War II Pilots on Their Final Mission

Bomb the cities to save them, the pillars of civilization —

Attack fiercely with firmness and might —

Whiisper: (kill women and children if need be to get the job done)

Your country will be proud of you when victory is won —

And God, He too, will be proud of you and with you all the way in this brave and noble task,

To wipe oppression from the earth and end all wars at last.

A Child's Question

Why should we do what we're told when those who tell us
what to do are rarely those who possess wisdom and speak
the truth, or those who never did what they were told or if
they did, did wiseless things they were told to do by wise-
less people who did what they were told by the command
of more wiseless people, and the core of their wishes lacks
sense and aim and direction and purpose and meaning
and things are never the way we're told they are, never turn
out the way they're supposed to, the way we're told they
will according to the dear wiseless people always telling us
what to do, so why should we do what we're told like
obedient little robots, like mindless-following sheep when
every generation before us has ultimately been a failure,
has mainly made a mess of things desecrating the miracle
of life with senseless bloodshed and madness spawned by
hate and greed and pettiness, consumed more and more
with the banal and superficial, always wanting, always
reaching for the next frivolous thing, just anything to
distract them, anything that will aid them in their perennial
task of fleeing from their boredom, from their fear, from
their wretchedness, from their evil, from *themselves* . . .
Oh tell us, yes please tell us why oh why we should listen
to the likes of you —

please do

Eavesdrop on a Lordly Debate

A. . . . yes, definitely evil, without doubt, without question.

B. But that's so negative what you say; no, no! I could never accept anything like that — the things you tell me about my dear human race. You see, we're not evil, no — just sometimes led astray, and 'Jesus loves me this I know, for the Bible tells me so' oh I wish you could see as I do, could feel His love, could only believe, then all would be right, so well and good; you'd see, for you and I and everyone who prays and believes, just put your trust in Him and His glory and we'll live happily ever after with Him in God's kingdom, He sitting at the right hand of the Father and we forever

A. on our knees and..

B. Pray to God, poor soul! Oh praise the Lord and do believe!

In This Human Race

There are those at the top and those at the bottom
who shouldn't be there, who seem out of place —
the former, deserving a lower rank, the latter,
worthy of a higher. But the ones in the middle . . .
they always seem well at home, like they truly belong —
the lukewarm middle-of-the-roaders being just
where they ought to be —

the jelly in the sandwich, so to speak

Earthquakes of a Life

Those earthquakes of a life taking everything under
destroying all, leaving nothing but its center —

The soul in its purest state —

The mind at its lightest weight —

At such times never so free

In – Sight

Yes, when that something happens finally, happens
powerfully in the all-of-a-sudden insight drawing near
to revelation, getting close then closer to those worthwhile
moments that send your sufferings back to you in waves of
bliss anointing your eyes with truths forged in fire invisible
your eyes then now to see in stunning clarity the meaning
of it all from whY to Be then gone almost as quickly as
they arrived but leaving their essence to stir in the nest
of your heart for the rest of your journey, through the
remainder of your life
when that something happens   happens . . .

Fears

running up man's back, over his head
leaping into the world running forever,
fleeing from Life   from Truth   from Terror —

rats chasing rats

Reactionary Lives

...always responding to .... never bringing forth

Birth of Spiritual Knowledge

Knowing that we know nothing —

N*othing* . . .

Only

When

Learning the depth of our ignorance and the immense folly of our

Ego can we free our consciousness and begin to grow, absorb, cultivate,

Define,

Get to the essence of the true, the real, the

Eternal . . .

only then

Not Always So Gently

... like the crocodile beast carrying her young
gently in her jaws capable of snapping thick logs
and cutting through bones of all prey, taking them
newly hatched from shore to water to shore
tender in her care ... Muse, the fertile beast moves
her brood from shore to spirit, from spirit to shore —

but not always so gently

The Spruce and the Pear Tree

The giant spruce stands near to the small pear tree
as barren of fruit and leaf as a tree can be at this
time of year, in this autumn month of November
the spruce fully dressed, standing tall and looking
splendid covered with foliage, so richly adorned
but never to bear fruit as the little pear tree has done
and will again do, though now looking so feeble
crouched over like an aged hunchback
its twined limbs gray and brittle
so barren and naked, dwarfed by the spruce's
great presence and beauty
but never will the spruce bear fruit for as long
as it stands, for as long as it lives, as the little
pear tree has done and will again do,
nourishing life with the gift of its bounty
in hues of green most beautiful.

At a Reading

Faces probing, reaching, trying to understand . . .
more beautiful than the words the poets are speaking

What Might the Greatest Poem Be?

A poem composed for a billion minds absorbing its insights all at once —

The face of humanity lighting like the stars

Reunion

OK . . . just for you; I'll tell you what I've been up to
I've been down in the mines; no, not the mines that come
to mind, the mines of the soul battling demons from dawn
to dusk day in, day out but time doesn't exist in such a
place, in such places as where I've been since last I saw
you but that's another story, something to be discussed
at another time, in another place and now may I tell you
you're looking fine, better than fine, quite well as a matter
of fact; the pain in your eyes becomes you . . . I see you're
in the process of becoming — a period of transformation
fueled by something from the kind of suffering that brings
growth and realization to the life in question if being lived
by someone of spiritual worth which you most certainly
are, friend and confidant of my youth, I would ask you to
join me for a spell but I see you've travelled far enough into
yourself to know that such things are really not possible . . .
yes, I've been working the mines, the mines of the soul to
which I must shortly return but shall we first join in a toast
wishing the world well *for it ofttimes seems like it's surely
going to hell* then gather images of each other before we part
to take with us on our way to separate destinies to make
the way a little sweeter, perhaps a little brighter (but not
easier) preserving our memories of this day, of this moment
somewhere in our pain, our joy, our love and the thousand
births and deaths our spirits are yet to experience
in our journey to journeys ahead . . .

Farewell, dear friend . . .
till we meet again

ABOUT THE AUTHOR

Carroll Blair is an award-winning author of more than twenty books. His work has been well endorsed and commendably reviewed, as illustrated by the following commentary from Midwest Review, which proclaimed, *"The poetic expression of Carroll Blair is both unique and compelling. Using word images like the strokes of a painter's brush, Blair creates a resonating recognition that is the mark of a master poet."*
He is an alumnus of the Boston Conservatory and lives in Massachusetts.

www.ingramcontent.com/pod-product-compliance
Lightning Source LLC
Chambersburg PA
CBHW020013050426
42450CB00005B/444